GW01336939

Find Out what your Structure is with your phone/browser

1. Go to **www.joeyyap.com/5s**

2. Key in your Date of Birth

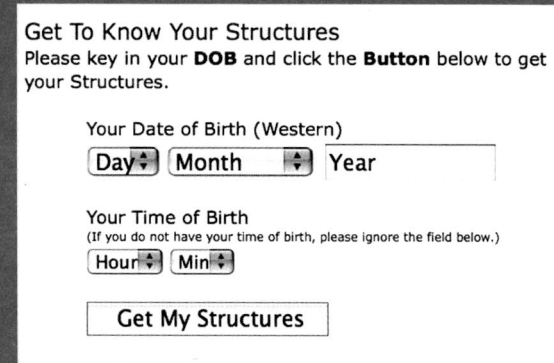

3. Your Structure is instantly revealed

Your Structure is:
SUPPORTERS
(Influence Structure)

* The calculator will automatically convert your Western date of birth to Chinese in deriving your Day Master

忠誠型

SUPPORTERS
(Influence Structure)

BaZi Essentials: The Five Structures
SUPPORTERS (Influence Structure)

Copyright © 2010 by Joey Yap
All rights reserved worldwide.
First Edition April 2010

All intellectual property rights contained or in relation to this book belongs to Joey Yap.

No part of this book may be copied, used, subsumed, or exploited in fact, field of thought or general idea, by any other authors or persons, or be stored in a retrieval system, transmitted or reproduced in any way, including but not limited to digital copying and printing in any form whatsoever worldwide without the prior agreement and written permission of the author.

The author can be reached at:

Mastery Academy of Chinese Metaphysics Sdn. Bhd. (611143-A)
19-3, The Boulevard, Mid Valley City,
59200 Kuala Lumpur, Malaysia.
Tel   : +603-2284 8080
Fax   : +603-2284 1218
Website : www.masteryacademy.com

DISCLAIMER:

The author, Joey Yap and the publisher, JY Books Sdn Bhd, have made their best efforts to produce this high quality, informative and helpful book. They have verified the technical accuracy of the information and contents of this book. Any information pertaining to the events, occurrences, dates and other details relating to the person or persons, dead or alive, and to the companies have been verified to the best of their abilities based on information obtained or extracted from various websites, newspaper clippings and other public media. However, they make no representation or warranties of any kind with regard to the contents of this book and accept no liability of any kind for any losses or damages caused or alleged to be caused directly or indirectly from using the information contained herein.

Published by JY Books Sdn. Bhd. (659134-T)

INDEX

1	**PERSONALITY**	17
a	**The Good**	21
	Even-tempered	22
	Keen Listener	24
	Amusing	26
	Compassionate	28
b	**The Bad**	31
	Inflexible	32
	Indifferent	34
	Sarcastic	36
	Judgmental	38
2	**PERSONALITY AS A PARENT**	41
a	**The Good**	42
	Involved	44
	Patient	46
	Balanced	48

b	**The Bad**	51
	Too relaxed	52
	Disorganised	54
	Too Lenient	56
3	**THE INFLUENCE STRUCTURE PERSONALITY AT A GLANCE**	59
a	**The Bright Side**	60
b	**The Dark Side**	64
4	**PERSONALITY AT WORK**	69
a	**The Good**	71
	Peacemaker	72
	Stable	74
	Empathetic	76
	Supportive	78

b	**The Bad**	81
	Passive	82
	Sneaky	84
	Lack urgency	86
	Indecisive	88
c	**Suitable Careers**	90
d	**Suitable Job Roles & Environment**	94
5	**WEALTH OUTLOOK**	99
a	**Obstacles to Wealth**	100
b	**Best path to Wealth**	104
6	**INTERACTING WITH INFLUENCE STRUCTURE PERSON**	109
7	**IDENTIFYING THE EXTREME INFLUENCE STRUCTURE PERSON**	115

MASTERY ACADEMY
OF CHINESE METAPHYSICS™

At **www.masteryacademy.com**, you will find some useful tools to ascertain key information about the Feng Shui of a property or for the study of Astrology.

The Joey Yap Flying Stars Calculator can be utilised to plot your home or office Flying Stars chart. To find out your personal best directions, use the 8 Mansions Calculator. To learn more about your personal Destiny, you can use the Joey Yap BaZi Ming Pan Calculator to plot your Four Pillars of Destiny – you just need to have your date of birth (day, month, year) and time of birth.

For more information about BaZi, Xuan Kong or Flying Star Feng Shui, or if you wish to learn more about these subjects with Joey Yap, logon to the Mastery Academy of Chinese Metaphysics website at **www.masteryacademy.com.**

Mastery Academy
E-Learning Center
www.maelearning.com

Bookmark this address on your computer, and visit this newly-launched website today. With the E-Learning Center, knowledge of Chinese Metaphysics is a mere 'click' away!

Our E-Learning Center consists of 3 distinct components.

1. Online Courses
These shall comprise of 3 Programs: our Online Feng Shui Program, Online BaZi Program, and Online Mian Xiang Program. Each lesson contains a video lecture, slide presentation and downloadable course notes.

2. MA Live!
With MA Live!, Joey Yap's workshops, tutorials, courses and seminars on various Chinese Metaphysics subjects broadcasted right to your computer screen. Better still, participants will not only get to see and hear Joey talk 'live', but also get to engage themselves directly in the event and more importantly, TALK to Joey via the MA Live! interface. All the benefits of a live class, minus the hassle of actually having to attend one!

3. Video-On-Demand (VOD)
Get immediate streaming-downloads of the Mastery Academy's wide range of educational DVDs, right on your computer screen. No more shipping costs and waiting time to be incurred!

Study at your own pace, and interact with your Instructor and fellow students worldwide...at your own convenience and privacy. With our E-Learning Center, knowledge of Chinese Metaphysics is brought DIRECTLY to you in all its clarity, with illustrated presentations and comprehensive notes expediting your learning curve!

Welcome to the Mastery Academy's E-LEARNING CENTER...
YOUR virtual gateway to Chinese Metaphysics mastery!

忠誠型

SUPPORTERS
(Influence Structure)

Empathetic, Loyal, Easy-going

The BaZi Structures: Knowing Your Place in the World

The idea for the **BaZi Essentials** series of books arose out of a desire to simplify the sophisticated study of Chinese Astrology into something a little easier to digest. Too many people are only familiar with the "12 Animal Year Signs" type of Chinese Astrology. But the true form of character traits in Chinese Astrology stems from the Day of Birth, not the Year of Birth. My previous series on the **BaZi Essentials: 10 Day Masters** focused on exactly that – the individual Day Master based on your Day of Birth.

If you've read my books on BaZi, **BaZi – The Destiny Code** and **BaZi – The Destiny Code Revealed**, or even taken any classes on the subject, you probably know that there is really NO end to BaZi studies. There may be a finite amount of theory or principles to learn, but the methods of application and interpretation are varying, complex, and hence, endless. That's precisely why BaZi can become a lifelong study and education.

The book you're currently holding in your hands belongs to the **BaZi Essentials: 5 Structures** series. It takes one step higher into demystifying the complex nature of BaZi studies to help you understand how you use BaZi your daily life, and to navigate through the events and people in your world.

But how is the **BaZi Structures** series book different from the Day Master series? Well, consider BaZi to have 3 layers of complexity based on the information gleaned from your day of birth:

10 Day Masters (Level 1)

<u>Who You Are</u> - The Day Master reveals your basic *character*; your essential personality traits, strengths and weaknesses fall under this.

5 Structures (Level 2)

<u>How You Approach the World</u> - The Structure reveals your personality *in relation* to the world. In essence, your BaZi Structure shows you your *modus operandi* – why you behave the way you do, and what attitudes you project in life.

10 Profiles (Level 3)

<u>What You Do</u> - The Profile reveals your individual lifestyle. It helps you understand what you do in the world, and how your actions are manifested. Your BaZi Profile explains your 'style' of operation in life. It's about how you function as a unique individual.

If you don't know what's your BaZi chart or your Structure, don't worry. You can log on to my website at www.joeyap.com/bazi5s to find out your Structure instantly.

It goes without saying that if you're an Influence Structure, you're obviously more than just the characteristics listed here. You're not only a quietly witty, sympathetic peacemaker who tries to avoid conflict and is consistently a follower, not a leader! This book will, however, provide you with a general blueprint as to how you approach your life.

What are your most negative and positive personality traits? What are you like as a friend, as a parent, and as a worker? What type of careers and job roles are best suited to your disposition, and how to you deal with everyday problems, challenges, and issues – whether in your professional or personal life? What is your attitude to wealth, and how would you best go about making the most of your talents to gain more wealth? In other words, what's your path of *least* resistance to wealth?

All these questions and more are addressed in this book, so that you're able to see exactly how the Influence Structure person is reacts to and interacts with external influences.

But bear in mind that in BaZi, the concept of STRONG or WEAK elements play a big role in determining how much of a Influence Structure you are. These factors are too varied and complex to be discussed here in a simple book (it is, however, a fundamental section of my professional BaZi courses and Destiny Code series of books). Suffice to say that to read and understand this particular book, you merely need to be aware of this concept. If your Structure is strong, you'll exhibit more of these tendencies outlined in this book.

The strongest element in your chart determines your BaZi Structure. However, it is entirely possible for one person to have a mix of Structures in his or her chart because of the different elements. As such, not everyone is a *pure* Structure. The second strongest element in your chart is known as your secondary BaZi Structure, and determines your secondary nature. Consider it your sub-behaviour, if you will. The print-out of your chart that you obtain from my website as mentioned above will clearly indicate the second strongest element.

A healthy BaZi Structure is one where the strengths of all the elements are balanced; one where a single element is not too strong. When an element is too strong, it becomes known as an extreme BaZi Structure. This is typically indicative that more of the negative traits of that particular structure will prevail.

You do need to bear in mind that this book shows you the traits of the Influence Structure *in general*, and doesn't take into account the particularities of your entire BaZi chart! Therefore, it also becomes extremely valuable and important to get a complete BaZi consultation from a professional, or to take a full BaZi course and learn and master the interpretation skills for your own individual use.

BaZi is a study that helps us understand ourselves, make better decisions, and ultimately, enables us to shape our life for the better. These compact, easy-to-understand guides are designed to help you fulfill your life's goals in a more meaningful way. I hope to make BaZi a relevant a part of your life – and may the knowledge that you gain serve you in all of life's endeavours.

I wish you much pleasure and excitement in your journey towards understanding BaZi and applying it in your life.

Joey Yap
April 2010

Author's personal website :
www.joeyyap.com

Academy websites :
www.masteryacademy.com | www.maelearning.com

Follow Joey Yap's current updates on Twitter :
www.twitter.com/joeyyap

Join Joey Yap on Facebook :
www.facebook.com/joeyyapFB

peng you

PERSONALITY

INTRODUCTION

Supporters

Influence Structure people are best described as being the supporters. They prop up other people, values, principles, or policies by diplomatic, easygoing nature. They are best described as being "the nice guys" of any workplace or group. They are amiable and eager to please, and consistently pleasant and inoffensive. They thrive in situations that are calm and stable. They are keen to minimise conflict with others and ensure that everyone is getting along.

Influence Structure people are very adept at following through with a game plan and a structure. Give them a proper framework to work within, and they will deliver the results (usually outstanding ones). They are also ideal mediators between people in conflict, whether friends, family, or colleagues, and will not trample over others to get to the top. They strive to work peaceably with others in order to get the job done, and are not interested in being competitive. Their primary concern is with caring for and guarding the feelings of others. They make ideal co-operators, and are unpretentious and low-key.

On the less positive side, however, Influence Structure people tend to lack initiative and drive, and will wait around to be given instructions before they embark upon anything. They are very good at following through with the plans, and dislike last-minute changes and alterations. They don't enjoy being in positions of power and leadership because this requires making decisions; and making decisions agitates them as they know that they might offend others.

hao

THE GOOD

忠誠型

SUPPORTERS Influence Structure

EVEN-TEMPERED
Laidback and takes things easy

Influence Structure people are very easy people to get along with. They tend to have a lot of friends because they inherently possess an inoffensive nature. They are inherently pleasant and kind-natured because they care about the feelings of others, and are careful not to hurt them.

Their naturally moderate nature means that they're able to walk the middle line better than most. They are naturally neutral and always aim for moderation. Influence Structure enjoys watching people, and finds it fascinating to learn about their quirks and personalities. As such, other people often feel welcome around Influence Structure.

Influence Structure people don't place unnecessary demands on their friends, and unlike certain other Structures who constantly need the attention and the spotlight, Influence Structure is content to be in the background, watching their friends shine. As such, their friendships with others are often free of resentment.

KEY FACTS

- **Inoffensive**
- **Moderate**
- **Pleasant and affable**
- **Non-demanding**

KEEN LISTENER
Attentive to friends' problems

The Influence Structure friend is a very good listener. They are always keen to know what their friends really think, and as such are always carefully inquiring after their friends' matters. More importantly, they are also keen to know the answer! Unlike other Structures who want to focus to turn back to themselves after awhile, Influence Structure is genuinely curious. They remain active listeners who absorb all that their friends have to say in the hopes of getting them to share their deepest troubles.

As such, the Influence Structure friend is the ideal person to head to with all of one's complaints! They are extremely patient and will not judge others for wanting to whine or vent. They understand the need for their friends to find a safe outlet for

their emotions, and hence make very good listeners because they don't interrupt or get their own two cents in all the time.

Also, because Influence Structure people don't need to be in the limelight or have all the attention focused on themselves, they are content to stay in the background. They rarely vie for attention among their friends, and so if their friends need them to listen, that's exactly what they'll do. Unlike the Output Structure, they won't be bored out of their minds after a few minutes, itching to tell their own stories and be the centre of attention again!

KEY FACTS

- **Attentive and curious**
- **Non-interfering**
- **Gives friends the space to express themselves**
- **Does not judge or interrupt**

AMUSING
Pleasing others with droll humour

Influence Structure people often appear placid and calm on the surface, and most people think of them as very bland! This is further emphasised by Influence Structure's penchant for being inoffensive and for valuing politeness and courtesy. However, what they do hide very well is their dry and witty sense of humour. When it comes out, watch out! This usually becomes more noticeable once they are comfortable with someone and have begun to trust them.

Influence Structure people get along with people because of this sense of humour. As they're often observant and watchful, they're able to make funny sense of everything that they see and perceive. In fact, there's nothing the Influence Structure

enjoys more than having a good laugh with close friends.

Influence Structure people are modest enough to know when to laugh at themselves when the situation calls for it. Some are so self-deprecating that making fun of themselves is a favourite past-time! However, they don't do this in a loud or slapstick way, as might be the style of the Output Structure. Influence Structure's humour is more self-contained and intelligent, and requires a bit of sophistication to be understood.

KEY FACTS

- Quietly witty
- Dry humour
- Ability to laugh at everything
- Self-deprecating

COMPASSIONATE
Always considering how others feel

Influence Structure people are known for being very compassionate because empathy is one of the traits they inherently possess. They are considerate of their friends' needs and troubles, and are able to step into their shoes to get an idea of what their friends are going through. They seek close, warm, and lasting relationships with others.

Influence Structure people will never fail to inquire about the wellbeing of their friends. With them, it's never all about "me, me, me!" They only feel deserving of talking about their own problems once they've ensured that their friends are not having any problems of their own. They extend themselves to others because of their need to please and their desire to make others happy.

Because of this, Influence Structure is able to win over many of their friends, and indeed often get loyal and devoted friends. Most of their friends know that Influence Structure's cause for concern is never a selfish one, or one motivated by materialistic desire. They may, however, pretend to consent even though they don't intend to consent simply because they're sensitive to other people's feelings and will not, as much to their ability, try to knowingly hurt others.

KEY FACTS

- **Sincere and kind**
- **Inquires after friends' wellbeing**
- **Ability to empathise**
- **Is not motivated by selfish purposes**

壞
huai

THE BAD

INFLEXIBLE
Resistant to change

On the whole, it can be said that Influence Structure people are quite resistant to change and upheaval. They like their routine and their stability; they feel better when things are going at a pace and in a direction in which they feel comfortable. They don't enjoy stepping out of their comfort zones. Inherently, they are not risk-takers because it disrupts their sense of peace.

Due to this nature, Influence Structure people can sometimes dampen their friends' spirits with their predilection for routine-based events. Their resistance to anything new means that they prefer to go to the same places to eat, have coffee, hang out. Also, they're not very enthusiastic about getting on board for different activities. If anything, Influence Structure likes to play it safe.

Influence Structure people like to revisit the same things over and over again, and it's no wonder that some of their friends find their preferences somewhat boring. After all, what's new about someone if you already know what they want and how they're going to do it? Influence Structure's refusal to be shaken out of its rut can be rather frustrating for its friends.

KEY FACTS
- **Resistant to change**
- **Stays in comfort zone**
- **Likes to follow a routine**
- **Can lead a humdrum existence**

INDIFFERENT
Refraining from being over-enthusiastic

Sometimes, all a friendship needs is some excitement and some energy. Don't, however, expect the Influence Structure person to provide it for its friends. As mentioned earlier, they prefer to traverse the well-known path and refrain trying out anything new. In addition to that, they can also be stubbornly indifferent.

Because of this, Influence Structure people can dampen the enthusiasm of any activity or project that their friends are involved in. They are likely to be quite the party-pooper. If and when someone thinks of something to do, and the Influence Structure person doesn't like, you can bet on their stodgy refusal to participate.

Instead of telling people what they don't want to do and what they dislike, Influence Structure may acquiesce at the start in order to avoid ruffling any feathers. But once something is embarked upon, they will prefer to sit out and will not participate, thereby ruining the atmosphere for everyone else!

KEY FACTS

- **Dampens enthusiasm**
- **Rains on the parade**
- **Refrain from getting involved**
- **Lacks excitement**

SARCASTIC
Having a sharp tongue

In extremely extreme or in unhealthy charts, Influence Structure people often have a very sharp tongue, and they tend to take out this sarcasm on people as a means of self defence. As such, their sense of humour can sometimes take on an edgier turn. What starts out as fun teasing can quickly becoming a veiled attack, or a snipe at their friends. While they try to pass off their sarcasm as humour, it can often hurt others.

Because Influence Structure relies a lot on its wit, they sometimes have trouble telling apart a witty joke from a sarcastic stab to the heart. Sarcasm in itself is not that cruel, but combined with Influence Structure's pent-up resentment, it can be quite the potent weapon.

Influence Structure people don't by nature intend to hurt others, but when they become defensive or feel as though they're being pushed into a corner, their cynical nature will rule. Sometimes, too, they may let what started out as a low-key, non-offensive joke to go overboard.

KEY FACTS

- Mocking
- Sardonic and cynical
- Mean-spirited humour at times
- Puts friends down with teasing

JUDGMENTAL
"This is the way it must be done"

Influence Structure people often have a rather rigid set of codes of conduct, or moral principles and values. Usually, they are upright people who value laws and rules, and often adhere to those same laws and rules. They consider civilisation to be built upon these socially-sanctioned laws.

However, sometimes Influence Structure people can impose their values and principles upon others. If other people fail to live up to it, they can become rather judgmental. They would prefer it if other people saw the world the way they did! They uphold the law and react very strongly to people or events that make them go against it.

This is largely because Influence Structure value their friends, and therefore hold them up to a higher standard than is perhaps realistic. Therefore, when their friends occasionally fall from grace, as does everyone, they are a lot more critical and negative about it than they usually would be. They also don't put friendships and relationships above the law or the rules. They're very critical of themselves if they don't follow the rules, and will judge others based on these pre-set rules as well.

KEY FACTS

- Critical
- Sets high moral standards
- Expects others to adhere to own standards
- Quick to judge someone else

fu mu

PERSONALITY AS A PARENT

hao

THE GOOD

INVOLVED
Taking the good with the bad

Influence Structure people make very good parents because they get very involved in their children's lives. They strive to make time for their children, and ensure that they are available as much as they can. They're very committed to being parents, and fully understand that they're in it for the long haul.

As such, Influence Structure parents always know where their children are at any given time, or what their likes and dislikes are, and who their friends are. There will rarely be a single facet of their children's lives that Influence Structure parents are unaware of – that is, until their children grow up to be teenagers!

Influence Structure parents are very good at carving out proper time and effort to care for their children. The bond that they have with their kids is very strong, and they will typically be the type of parents to drop everything else in order to attend to their family first. They are extremely concerned about their children's lives, and make sure to stay on top of it in every aspect.

KEY FACTS

- Committed
- Concerned parents
- Good at parenting
- Keen participant of their children's lives

PATIENT
Steady through the good and the bad

Children typically require a lot of patience, and who better to deal with this than the Influence Structure parent? By nature, Influence Structure people have great capacities for tolerance and endurance, and are therefore a little more patient than most people. As parents, this quality stands them in good stead. They are usually able to weather all sorts of tantrums and distractions on the part of their children!

Influence Structure parents are the kind who can tolerate their kids' misdemeanours in a lenient manner, as well. Instead of resorting to yelling or spanking as a quick fix, the Influence Structure parent is willing to talk it out with his or her kids and is able to put in the time that it takes to help their children learn a moral lesson. They will not be the parents who 'lose it' at every other opportunity!

Because of this, their children often feel safe and comfortable around them. Influence Structure parents are also willing to entertain endless questions and queries about the nature of the world, and are extremely accommodating of the incessant "Whys?" that young kids are so fond of asking. They don't like to rush their kids through life, and refrain from saying, "Hurry up" every time their children lag behind or take their time. As such, they help their children feel calm and at peace with the world with the patience and tolerance they reflect in their behaviour.

KEY FACTS

- **Tolerant**
- **Lenient**
- **Accommodating to children's needs**
- **Doesn't rush kids through life**
- **Helps children feel centred and calm**

BALANCED
No extremes of mood or temper

Influence Structure parents excel at walking the tightrope of emotions brought upon by parenthood. Their natural inclination is to be moderate. Their personality is such that they're unused to sudden extremes and emotional pendulum swings. This prepares them very well for the sudden changes brought upon by the world of parenting. They are extremely balanced and fair parents.

As such, Influence Structure parents make excellent impartial judges in the fights and arguments among their children. They don't take sides or play favourites, and will never judge a child unfairly. Furthermore, they behave in the same manner towards their own children. They treat them in a fair manner, and don't throw around their weight in authority just because they're the parents.

Influence Structure parents are very good at making their kids see right from wrong through example. They refrain from letting mood swings or emotional disturbances influence the way they treat their children. They try to maintain an even keel with their children, and don't allow themselves to get too upset too easily. Influence Structure parents are pro at taking both the good and the bad with equilibrium!

KEY FACTS

- **Fair and impartial**
- **Respects own children**
- **Doesn't let emotions influence parenting**
- **Strives to be just in dealing with all children**
- **Doesn't take sides or play favourites**

huai

THE BAD

TOO RELAXED
Hoping the home regulates itself

As Influence Structure people are fundamentally laid-back and relaxed, they don't tend to make plans or goals for their own life although they might be methodical while at work. But in personal living, they tend to take things one day at a time and have a 'play-it-by-ear' mentality. They would prefer to coast along without rocking the boat or upsetting too many apple carts.

Unfortunately, this same tendency tends to be at odds with their role of being a parent. Influence Structure parents are sometimes too lax with their rules and regulations even while they expect their children to adhere to high standards of behaviour. This causes frustration and disappointment for all involved, because while they're firm with the rules, they don't know how to be firm in implementing it. The

result is often contradictory behaviour, and sometimes, confusion.

If there are problems that crop up, Influence Structure parents tend to hope that these issues blow off on their own. They tend to take life a little too easy, and overlook some of the domestic issues or tensions that need to be addressed. As such, they may inadvertently ignore some serious problems – not through negligence, but through too much of a commitment to being laid-back.

KEY FACTS
- **Overly laid-back**
- **Hopes problems solve itself**
- **Don't take proactive measures**
- **May overlook serious problems**

DISORGANISED
No sense of a system

While Influence Structure people don't actually like living in a mess, they're not very good at enforcing some kind of organisational system in their home that prevents a mess. As such, they tend to run a very disorganised home as parents. Again, they tend to hope that other people will do the organising for them!

As parents, Influence Structure tends to have a hard time staying on top of their children's activities and schedules. They may double-book their children's appointments, or forget about important meetings. Sometimes, if the situation gets too bad, there can be calamity on the domestic front.

A significant part of the problem is Influence Structure's lack of commitment to getting its act together. As parents, they don't take the initiative to run their house in proper order or to provide a sense of structure to simple things like filing the household bills, keeping medical documents in an easy to reach place, and managing time well. As such, their sense of disorganisation sometimes leads to a helter-skelter type of life for their kids.

KEY FACTS

- Lacks structure
- Doesn't prioritise organisation
- Prefers to leave it to others
- Doesn't set out to solve problems

忠誠型

SUPPORTERS Influence Structure

TOO LENIENT
Giving their kids too much leeway

Influence Structure's sense of laidback living can sometimes turn out to be a bad thing in terms of parenting. They find it difficult to implement a system, as they like to follow a structure. In families, especially Asian families, where generations have adhered to strict traditions and guidelines, Influence Structure parents tend to do well. But if they have to do it by scratch, they end up with being afraid to push too hard, and thus allow their children to get away with too much.

Sometimes, their own compassion or "I feel bad" syndrome threatens to become rather compulsive, and therefore they allow their children to get away with bad behaviour rather than upset them and set some ground rules. Influence Structure parents never know when to say stop, and how to set boundaries.

When they do want to implement some sense of order, however, they can do it in a way that is tiring and exhausting for their children. Influence Structure parents tend to nag, and explain the rules over and over again, or ask their children, "Why are you doing this?" repeatedly until they get their children to do as they say!

KEY FACTS

- **Too lenient**
- **Doesn't set ground rules**
- **Tends to spoil children**
- **Allows overwhelming compassion to get in the way**

THE INFLUENCE STRUCTURE PERSONALITY AT A GLANCE

THE BRIGHT SIDE

優點

you dian

• Cooperative

You are always willing to work with others, and indeed, strive hard to attain team goals and fulfill productivity. You are good at carrying out instructions that have been assigned to a team or a group, and filling out the blanks in a structured organisation.

• Reliable

You can always be counted upon to finish things. You'll never leave a thread hanging and then escape. You are accountable for all that you do, finish tasks well ahead of time, and can be responsible for what you've taken on within the set boundaries.

• Sympathetic

You're always the one people turn to with a problem. If you find yourself often complaining that people come to you with all their problems and the kitchen sink – it's probably best to let your displeasure be known directly to them!

• Diplomatic

You're a much-needed referee in a work environment that's filled with eager rats ready to race to the top. Cut-throat office politics is just not your style if it means having to cut others down. You would much rather try to calm things down and play the peacemaker.

• Considerate

Consideration is your middle name, but consider how being considerate can hurt you. You're so busy minding other people's feelings, but are you aware of what you're feeling?

• Easygoing

Nothing much rattles you easily. You prefer to take the view that everything has its place and time, and therefore everything will sort itself out eventually. You're rarely barking out orders or screaming at someone for making a mistake. You maintain your perspective through it all and take things one thing at a time.

• Introspective

You're rarely to be found hogging the limelight, or talking the loudest. If anything, you're more inward-focused, and prefer to let others take their time and turn in the spotlight before coming forward with your opinion.

• Calm

There are rarely any hysterical extremities of feeling where you're concerned. You always walk the middle ground, and present a balanced worldview to everyone else. Usually, others tend to find you the calm in the storm, or a much-needed oasis in the desert.

• Tolerant

Far from the type of harried souls who rush things at the last-minute and demand from others things that were "due yesterday", you have the patience of the saint. You recognise that sometimes, good things take time. You are very tolerant and will get things done if required, and in the workplace, stay on overtime to do it if need be.

THE DARK SIDE

ruo dian

- **Pushover**

Don't let others think you lack a backbone. It's a sure-fire way to get the ruthless types to step all over you when and where they see fit. If you yourself sometimes feel that you lack a backbone, now is the right time to grow one!

- **Non-competitive**

While you may be fine with being non-competitive, you need to learn that getting ahead sometimes means getting ahead of someone else. That doesn't necessarily make you a horrible person by default. You tend to lose out on achieving your ambitions by refraining to be non-competitive on all fronts.

• Indecisive

You're the one saying, "Wherever is fine" when people are deciding on where to eat. It's time to reclaim your right to say, "No, I hate Burger King," and venture forth with a sound decision or opinion. People will respect you more when you actually demand for what you want.

• Rigid

If you're constantly adhering to 'The Plan,' it may be time to take a step back and stop adhering to it. You'll never know just what you're capable of until you venture off from predictable and familiar territory. Sometimes, rules are meant to be broken.

• Evasive

You're always avoiding having to tell someone something unpleasant to their face. But that's not always going to work. Practice being frank with people you really dislike. It doesn't matter whether or not they care because you don't care what they think!

• Procrastinator

Dawdling is fine when you're meant to dawdle, like when on vacation. But you know you need to step up when something is 'urgent' and you're still sipping a cup of coffee and enjoying your breakfast of doughnuts.

• Self-righteous

You are very principled and have a set of standards to which you adhere. However, you tend to force those same standards upon others. Not everyone needs to be the same, and people have different reasons for doing what they do.

事業
shi yue

PERSONALITY AT WORK

hao

THE GOOD

PEACEMAKER
The nice guys of the workplace

People of the Influence Structure are invariably the nice guys and girls of the workplace, or the amiable backroom person. They are constantly finding ways to like others and, as a result, are often the likable ones in the workplace. Generally, their main concern is with creating a conducive and harmonious environment where everyone gets along, or indeed, much like that famous 80's sitcom *Cheers*, "where everybody knows your name."

Influence Structure individuals are inherently diplomatic. They will try to find the middle ground in any situation, and as such can be considered the peacemaker because they tend to minimise conflict with other people, and between other people. In an office filled with large egos all aiming to put the other in

its place, the Influence Structure person is a breath of fresh air who thinks of everyone, not just his or herself.

They are the go-to people for most problems and complaints. They are consensus-driven and seek to minimise differences and maximise shared traits or universalities. They will not behave in any extreme manner that threatens the integrity of the workplace, or go all out to display his or her talents in a way that others find threatening. It's all about not upsetting the apple cart.

KEY FACTS

- **Harmonious**
- **Amiable**
- **Consensus-driven**
- **Diplomatic**

SUPPORTERS Influence Structure

忠誠型 Influence Structure

STABLE
"I am the rock"

Influence Structure people are not the flaky, flighty types who are there one minute then gone the next. In the workplace, you always know where you'll be able to find them. They are rock-steady in all that they do, and will rarely step out of line simply to prove a point or to annoy someone else. They are perfectly reliable individuals who can be counted on to see things through till the end.

Others often find that people of the Influence Structure are there for them in the workplace and for that reason others often gravitate to the Influence Structure to help them sort out conflicts. In this scenario, Influence Structures are not prone to having extremes of temper and mood, and rarely ever take this out on the people around them.

Rest assured that the Influence Structure individual is rarely the type to cop a diva attitude simply to push for his or her own selfish interests. They are very measured and precise in their methods and actions, and as such inspire a sense of steadiness among others around them as well. They are thorough and take their time to get to the heart of the matter before proceeding.

KEY FACTS

- Reliable
- Will not rock the boat
- Precise
- Measured and thorough

EMPATHETIC
Sensitive to others' feelings

Influence Structure individuals are not the heartless, ruthless, competitive types who are out to slay everyone else who gets in their way. Indeed, because of their lack of a competitive edge, they are often considerate and thoughtful individuals who often put the interests of others ahead of their own. As such, other people will find them considerate people who are sensitive to the needs of others.

In a competitive environment, they are very careful about hurting the feelings of others, or making other people feel inferior or worthless in any way. That is simply not their style. As such, Influence Structure people will frequently let other people win or get ahead in the interests of preserving a friendship or professional bond.

Influence Structures are very people-centric. A healthy work environment for them means one that where the people feel secure, fulfilled and content; not one where everyone is feeling edgy and insecure and ready to claw each other's eyes out. This may seem like a common desire, but there are plenty of people who thrive in environments of fragile egos and bruised feelings! The Influence Structure person is not one of them. As such, they are often remembered or recalled as being kind and thoughtful.

KEY FACTS

- **Caring**
- **People-first attitude**
- **Doesn't enjoy hurting others' feelings**
- **Unselfish**

SUPPORTIVE
Carrying the weight of the workplace

If an Influence Structure person is 100% behind a cause, person, or company, they will throw all of themselves into their work and will be very supportive. In that sense, they are like the pillars that keep the roof of a building where it's supposed to be – not crumbling down to the floor! They are focused on what's best for everyone involved, not just themselves.

As such, they make perfect supporters and can be very cooperative in fulfilling the goals of a company or project. Because they care about people, they value the fruits of genuine and supportive teamwork, as well, and will go all-out to cultivate an environment that makes everyone feel comfortable. They can be incredibly patient, and will sometimes be too lenient in waiting as long as it takes for someone else to finish the job!

Because they empathise and sympathise a lot with others, they can be incredibly loyal and an advent supporter once their trust has been won. As such, bosses and managers may find the Influence Structure individual useful in rallying others around a cause if there seems to be a problem in arriving at a consensus. Their cooperative nature means that they will find ways to work with others – their instinct is to work together, not to work at odds or in conflict.

KEY FACTS

- **Accommodating**
- **Team-work centred**
- **Doesn't step out of line**
- **Cooperative and focused**

huai

THE BAD

PASSIVE
"Tell me what to do and I'll do it"

On the flip side, when the Influence Structure's key qualities manifest themselves negatively, they can be alarmingly and annoyingly passive in all that they do. What this means is that they'll do what they have to (remember, they'll never rock the boat in any major way), but they will not innovate or do more than what they're expected to from the start.

Influence Structure is very good at toeing the line and following instructions. They will do what they're asked or ordered to do, but will not take the initiative to come up with new solutions or bear responsibility for something out of the ordinary than what they're used to. This means that others will often have a hard time getting Influence Structure people to kick-start something all on their own.

As such, Influence Structure is very easy to supervise, but very hard to inspire or motivate to lead. They respond very well to a game plan, but expect them to get things done on their own without any supervision and it will be a losing battle. They will only get going when they is a clear plan already outlined, or a task clearly delineated from start to finish.

KEY FACTS
- Lack initiative
- Following rather than leading
- Needs supervision
- Submissive

SNEAKY
Not to your face, but behind your back

Being sneaky may seem at odds with the Influence Structure's capacity for kindness and consideration, but it is the other end of the spectrum – when their niceness is taken too far, or to an extreme. When this happens, they care too much about wanting to preserve good ties – even if it's an illusion – and worry too much about offending or upsetting another person. The Influence Structure individual hates conflict.

As such, if they're unhappy about something, they will complain about the situation behind your back, not to your face. They will very rarely march up to you and tell you what's wrong. They won't own up to their unhappiness or their source of conflict, and will find it easier to go around the problem than actually address it. These are

the people who will much rather pretend that the big purple elephant in the middle of the sitting room in simply *not* there.

This precise attitude can frustrate others, especially people who are blunt and forthright and would rather get things out in the open. The Influence Structure person will rather cover their behinds than engage in a long or potentially drawn-out conflict that they feel will upset the apple cart, rock the boat, or ruffle some feathers. This is a big no-no for the Influence Structure!

KEY FACTS

- **Behind-the-back type person**
- **Not forthright**
- **Fear of confrontation**
- **Fear of offending others**

LACKS URGENCY
What's the rush?

Influence Structure individuals also have significant problems with time management. They're too concerned with ensuring that things go right that they sometimes lose focus on ensuring that they're own tasks are going right! More importantly, they lack a sense of urgency and tend to be similar to the Resource Structure in terms of being thorough, methodical and precise.

As such, these are not the individuals to turn to when you need something in a rush. They may promise to deliver something and that use delaying tactics to stall matters further because they know they can't finish it on time. Urgent matters are never merely urgent to the Influence Structure. To them, there is always more time to do it later!

But the main reason for this is their poor sense of time management. Because they don't take the initiative to see how to improve things, they tend to coast by on old methods and stale tricks because "it has always worked." This can sometimes cost them dearly when they need to adapt to new methods or switch up things and find that they are unable to do so.

KEY FACTS

- Lack time management
- Don't see a need for urgency
- Tend to stick to rigid ways
- Don't improvise on methods

INDECISIVE
Or rather, fear of being decisive

Another key flaw among Influence Structure types is their lack of courage in being able to make a decision. Part of this stems from their need to please. Making a decision means taking a stand, and making a stand means ruffling some feathers while pleasing others. And what is it that the Influence Structure can't stand to do? Yes. Ruffle any feathers.

If they learned that one can't always be pleasing everybody, they'd be more decisive and better at leading and taking a stand. But Influence Structures are often caught in a trap of wanting to please and be non-offensive, which is inherently self-defeating as *no one* is able to be that way, all the time. In order to do it, one must care a little less about things, and become more passive.

Others will find that there's no point asking the Influence Structure for honest or critical advice or feedback because they will very rarely get it. Influence Structure people tend to sugar-coat their words in their attempt to present a bland and non-offensive front, but this rarely proves helpful or in any way constructive. As such, working with the Influence Structure person means that one may have to be prepared to repeatedly go over the same issues.

KEY FACTS

- **Waffling over decisions**
- **Rarely takes a stand**
- **Sugar-coats advice and feedback**
- **Will not take the responsibility/lead**

SUITABLE CAREER

- **Law Enforcement**

Influence Structures are primed for following the rules and instituting the rules. Their natural and inherent respect for social norms and mores, and more importantly, the laws and rules that govern any community, is a decisive strength when they work in law enforcement – whether in supervisory roles or directly as law enforcement personnel. They don't have to be made to respect the law – they already do. As such, they will bring a high level of integrity to their job.

- **Management and Administration**

The Influence Structure individual's propensity for keeping things structured and well-ordered makes them ideal candidates for management and administration roles in corporations. Once there is a clear plan to adhere to, they will ensure that everyone adheres to it. In addition, their ability to play nice and be diplomatic peacemakers ensures their commitment to treating everyone fairly and maintaining a safe and comfortable working environment for all. They will rarely be motivated by personal greed or selfish, political ambitions.

- **Human Resource**

As the Influence Structure's major interest and motivation is people, human resource is a sound avenue for their talents and skills. They naturally gravitate towards finding the peaceable middle ground for employees in a workplace, without sacrificing adherence to employer's rules and policies. Also, their ability to empathize and their sensitivity stand them in good stead, along with their ability to be patient and tolerant. Their natural propensity for precise, measured methods and actions while also valuing the principles of teamwork makes them the ideal go-to person for interpersonal and employee issues at the workplace.

- **Teachers, Educators**

The Influence Structure is very patient and easygoing, and will not get frustrated at having to explain things over and over again. As such, they make very accommodating and pleasant teachers, and present a non-threatening stance towards their students. They are also incredibly supportive and will be a very nurturing figure, in addition to being empathetic and considerate of their students' needs.

SUITABLE JOB ROLES & ENVIRONMENT

- **A game plan to follow through**

   Influence Structure people can't be thrown into the deep end of the water and expected to swim. They need to be provided a floating device. Likewise, at the workplace, they can't be expected to play it by ear and go with the flow... as the flow flows. No, they need a detailed guide that they can execute and fulfill to perfection. Their need to be measured, thorough, and precise doesn't allow for spontaneous changes and last-minute surprises.

- **Less competition, more kumbaya around the campfire**

  Well, not really. While there is no need to officially institute campfire hours where employees sit around holding hands and singing songs to guitar-playing, it is important that a harmonious, peaceful work environment is in place. Influence Structures find their strengths and talents maximised and brought to fruition when people are getting along, and there is no in-fighting and rampant office politics. Working in a place where egos are more important than the work involved is a sure-fire cause of depression for the Influence Structure.

- **AVOID: A leadership role that requires decision-making**

  The Influence Structure will not thrive in situations where they are expected to be in a decision-making process for a greater percentage of the time. They are followers, not leaders, and there's nothing wrong with that. Plenty of corporations and successful enterprises need sensitive, meticulous people who will adhere to the plan when the need calls for it. Plenty of people aren't willing to do that, but Influence Structure people are.

  Therefore, in order to help them thrive, they need to work in situations where they are made to execute a plan or a strategy. They will also perform better if they're made to use their peacemaking skills to help maintain a conducive environment in the office. Influence Structure people work better when they, like anyone else, are put to use for their actual talents, as opposed to subsuming them to fit into a cut-throat corporate culture.

财富
cai fu

WEALTH OUTLOOK

OBSTACLES TO WEALTH

- One of the main problems faced by the Influence Structure in terms of wealth attainment is their inability to take risks and step out of their comfort zone. This is a large part of being able to acquire wealth.

- They also tend to make wealth attainment a very difficult process for themselves by setting very high goals, or too many 'rules' that they need to get around. They set up roadblocks for themselves by saying things like, "I need to get a degree before I can do this," or "I need to find a guarantor or else I can't". They're so concerned with adhering to the proper guidelines that they miss the opportunities to slip in through the cracks and make a killing.

- Influence Structure people also lack courage to create a structure. They need to work on pre-planned, pre-existing guidelines. But making one up on their own is too risky for them. Even while they might have the creativity or the ideas, they're too afraid it won't work, and will rather rely on tried-and-tested methods that might not be the best option for them.

- Influence Structure also lacks urgency in seeing things through. To truly be available to wealth opportunities, one needs to be able to suss out potential opportunities and make a quick decision when the need arises. This means acting fast.

- Influence Structure people also have a hard time making decisions and sticking by it – a crucial factor in making choices that lead to possible monetary profit. Shying away from making a stand in fear of offending or unpleasing others does not pave the path to riches.

BEST PATHS TO WEALTH

- Influence Structure individuals will do well to find job stability and financial comfort through jobs and roles that allow them to exercise their predilection for caring for people, and maintaining a sense of structure and due process.

- As such, they work well as skilled professionals in whatever field that they're into – whether they be doctors, accountants, or in a field or scope of work that allows them to practice and serve others using their skills, without having to juggle other responsibilities.

- People who have made it big on their nice-guy status are John F. Kennedy and Bill Clinton. They have achieved fame and status exactly by parlaying their "people-first" charm and propensity for kindness into a bona fide industry of likeable-ness.

- If Influence Structure can tap into its skills and go all out in starting something new, he or she can make money by being a visionary in their field. Some examples of this are Michael Bloomberg and Bill Gates.

Famous Influence Structure People

- Michael Bloomberg
- *Bill Gates (Extreme Influence Structure)
- John F. Kennedy
- Steven Spielberg
- John F. Kennedy. Jr

NOTE: However, this is a very rare and intense scenario. Influence Structure is a little different from the other structures in that, in some extreme cases, they become audacious risk-takers with a do-or-die mentality, becoming fiercely competitive and ambitious and very dynamic. This is when they manifest the Seven Killings quality (which is one of the 10 Profiles that will be featured in the upcoming BaZi Essentials: 10 Profiles books)

INTERACTING WITH THE INFLUENCE STRUCTURE PERSON

SUPPORTERS Influence Structure

忠誠型

If you know people who belong to the Influence Structure and want to know how to best work with them (as colleagues) and manage them (as an employer), read on for some hints:

- The best way to deal with an Influence Structure personality is through informal, personable settings. The environment needs to be free of 'pressure' in order to make them comfortable and receptive enough to your suggestions.

- Maintain ample physical space between yourself and the Influence Structure person. Don't crowd their space – it's tantamount to launching an aggressive attack, in their eyes.

- Don't force their hand. They will only retreat. In fact, it's best to not expect much from them to begin with – or pretend that you don't expect much. When they feel free of expectations, they will be more inclined to take a risky step forward.

- They respect rules and structures, up to a point. So, getting an Influence Structure person to see things your way, or getting them to do things, will be easier if you can recite these rules to them and present the facts behind it to win them over. Be methodical, systematic, and lay down the ground rules right from the very beginning.

SUPPORTERS Influence Structure

忠誠型

- Don't, god forbid, take the hard approach or resort to emotional extremes and hysterical manipulation.

- It's important to outline the game plan from the start and then to stick to it. Changing things midstream will not be good, as they cannot handle last-minute changes. Doing so will only make them further frustrated, and lead to more delays and indecisiveness. Respect their need for structure.

- The kind approach works wonders. Influence Structure individuals are often sensitive and relate to others through sympathy and empathy. So be less brutal and up-front in your dealings with them. Circumvent around the issue first with overtures of niceties – and it will help if this can be cultivated sincerely!

IDENTIFYING THE EXTREME INFLUENCE STRUCTURE PERSON

At the workplace, it will be fairly easy to spot the Influence Structure person with extreme qualities. Read on to find out how these qualities are manifested:

忠誠型

SUPPORTERS Influence Structure

The Submissive

- He has a strong need for acceptance and support, and portrays a reasonable amount of support in public. However, he may be a totally different person in private. He accepts responsibility, but doesn't follow through. At the last-minute or at a critical juncture, he will likely drop the ball.

Deal with it by:
Taking his feelings into consideration, but asking him for a definite opinion if it's needed in a particular conflict or issue. Don't do this by forcing his hand in front of others. Speak with him privately, in a non-threatening environment. He is more likely to respond then.

- He is keen not to offend anyone. As such, he will acquiesce to your views or demands and say yes to any of your requests. However, because he knows he can't deliver, he will resort to delaying tactics or keep offering excuses as to why he can't finish it instead of telling you straight up.

Deal with it by:
Setting strict deadlines and drawing up a step-by-step plan with him on how to proceed. Then, follow up on those steps by constantly checking in on the progress. If at any point he can't finish it due to a particular reason, you'll be aware of it before the deadline – and can work with him to fix it.

忠誠型

SUPPORTERS Influence Structure

- He is completely unenthusiastic about most things, and prefers not to get involved. Or else, he pretends to be that way so that no one will give him more responsibilities. He will shy away from taking on more duties and tasks in order to avoid these responsibilities.

Deal with it by:
Starting small, as you must with all things. Give him minor responsibilities and keep it low-key – don't announce to others if possible. Allow him to have the space to make mistakes, and avoid heaping too much pressure (or enthusiasm) upon him. Then, gradually get him used to the idea of taking on more. Don't throw it all at him at once.

- He never lets you know if he's displeased with you, or anyone else. However, he does complain about everyone behind their back. He has lots of dissatisfactions, but he never says it to anyone's face. He is constantly griping about it to everyone else but the people involved.

Deal with it by:
Confronting him, but gently. If you know he's been talking about you, or if you're his supervisor and you want to confront him about his griping about colleagues, talk to him directly. Keep your emotions out of the way. If he's unhappy with you, the only way to get him to talk is for you to act neutrally, not defensively. That's the only way to get him to open up, and for you to ascertain if his complaints are legitimate.

Further Your BaZi Knowledge
Recommended Reading and Courses

Must-have BaZi Basics!

BaZi – The Destiny Code provides complete beginners knowledge on the fundamentals of BaZi in clear, easy-to-understand language and vivid examples, while BaZi – The Destiny Code Revealed is an in-depth resource on advanced BaZi principles and theories.

1) BaZi – The Destiny Code

2) BaZi – The Destiny Code Revealed

WWW.MASTERYACADEMY.COM/ESTORE

Study BaZi from the Comforts of Your Home

Supplement your BaZi studies from home with our online courses. Video lectures by Joey Yap, combined with slide presentations and notes, provide you with a complete BaZi learning experience. All without having to step outside your door!

WWW.MAELEARNING.COM/BZONLINE

Study BaZi at the Mastery Academy

Embark on BaZi classes at the Mastery Academy with Joey Yap and our team of professional instructors. Learn the ancient techniques and secrets in an intimate, friendly setting, aided by professional teaching tools and workbooks. Practical training and a conducive learning environment!

Design Your Destiny

Module One   – Intensive Foundation Course
Module Two   – Practitioners Course
Module Three – Advanced Practitioners Course
Module Four   – BaZi Mastery

WWW.MASTERYACADEMY.COM

About Joey Yap

Joey Yap is the founder of the Mastery Academy of Chinese Metaphysics, a global organization devoted to the teaching of Feng Shui, BaZi, Mian Xiang and other Chinese Metaphysics subjects. He is also the Chief Consultant of Yap Global Consulting, an international consulting firm specialising in Feng Shui and Chinese Astrology services and audits.

Joey Yap is the bestselling author of over 30 books on Feng Shui, Chinese Astrology, Face Reading and Yi Jing, many of which have topped the Malaysian and Singaporean MPH bookstores' bestseller lists.

Thousands of students from all around the world have learnt and mastered Classical Feng Shui, Chinese Astrology, and other Chinese Metaphysics subjects through Joey Yap's structured learning programs, books and online training. Joey Yap's courses are currently taught by over 30 instructors worldwide.

Every year Joey Yap conducts his 'Feng Shui and Astrology' seminar to a crowd of more than 3500 people at the Kuala Lumpur Convention Center. He also takes this annual seminar on a world tour to Frankfurt, San Francisco, New York, Toronto, London, Sydney and Singapore.

In addition to being a regular guest on various radio and TV shows, Joey Yap has also written columns for The New Straits Times and The Star - Malaysia's two leading newspapers. He has also been featured in many popular global publications and networks like Time International, Forbes International, the International Herald Tribune and Bloomberg.

He has also hosted his own TV series, 'Discover Feng Shui with Joey Yap', on 8TV, a local Malaysian network in 2005; and 'Walking The Dragons with Joey Yap' on Astro Wah Lai Toi, Malaysia's cable network in 2008.

Joey Yap has worked with HSBC, Bloomberg, Microsoft, Samsung, IBM, HP, Alliance, Great Eastern, Citibank, Standard Chartered, OCBC, SIME UEP, Mah Sing, Auto Bavaria, Volvo, AXA, Singtel, ABN Amro, CIMB, Hong-Leong, Manulife and others.

Author's personal website :www.joeyyap.com

Follow Joey Yap's regular updates on Twitter:

 www.twitter.com/joeyyap

Join Joey Yap on Facebook:

 **www.facebook.com/JoeyYapFB**

EDUCATION
The Mastery Academy of Chinese Metaphysics:
the first choice for practitioners and aspiring students of the art and science of Chinese Classical Feng Shui and Astrology.

For thousands of years, Eastern knowledge has been passed from one generation to another through the system of discipleship. A venerated master would accept suitable individuals at a young age as his disciples, and informally through the years, pass on his knowledge and skills to them. His disciples in turn, would take on their own disciples, as a means to perpetuate knowledge or skills.

This system served the purpose of restricting the transfer of knowledge to only worthy honourable individuals and ensuring that outsiders or Westerners would not have access to thousands of years of Eastern knowledge, learning and research.

However, the disciple system has also resulted in Chinese Metaphysics and Classical Studies lacking systematic teaching methods. Knowledge garnered over the years has not been accumulated in a concise, systematic manner, but scattered amongst practitioners, each practicing his/her knowledge, art and science, in isolation.

The disciple system, out of place in today's modern world, endangers the advancement of these classical fields that continue to have great relevance and application today.

At the Mastery Academy of Chinese Metaphysics, our Mission is to bring Eastern Classical knowledge in the fields of metaphysics, Feng Shui and Astrology sciences and the arts to the world. These Classical teachings and knowledge, previously shrouded in secrecy and passed on only through the discipleship system, are adapted into structured learning, which can easily be understood, learnt and mastered. Through modern learning methods, these renowned ancient arts, sciences and practices can be perpetuated while facilitating more extensive application and understanding of these classical subjects.

The Mastery Academy espouses an educational philosophy that draws from the best of the East and West. It is the world's premier educational institution for the study of Chinese Metaphysics Studies offering a wide range and variety of courses, ensuring that students have the opportunity to pursue their preferred field of study and enabling existing practitioners and professionals to gain cross-disciplinary knowledge that complements their current field of practice.

Courses at the Mastery Academy have been carefully designed to ensure a comprehensive yet compact syllabus. The modular nature of the courses enables students to immediately begin to put their knowledge into practice while pursuing continued study of their field and complementary fields. Students thus have the benefit of developing and gaining practical experience in tandem with the expansion and advancement of their theoretical knowledge.

Students can also choose from a variety of study options, from a distance learning program, the Homestudy Series, that enables study at one's own pace or intensive foundation courses and compact lecture-based courses, held in various cities around the world by Joey Yap or our licensed instructors. The Mastery Academy's faculty and make-up is international in nature, thus ensuring that prospective students can attend courses at destinations nearest to their country of origin or with a licensed Mastery Academy instructor in their home country.

The Mastery Academy provides 24x7 support to students through its Online Community, with a variety of tools, documents, forums and e-learning materials to help students stay at the forefront of research in their fields and gain invaluable assistance from peers and mentoring from their instructors.

MASTERY ACADEMY
OF CHINESE METAPHYSICS

www.masteryacademy.com

MALAYSIA
19-3, The Boulevard, Mid Valley City, 59200 Kuala Lumpur, Malaysia
Tel : +603-2284 8080   Fax : +603-2284 1218   Email : info@masteryacademy.com

Australia, Austria, Canada, China, Croatia, Cyprus, Czech Republic, Denmark, France, Germany, Greece, Hungary, India, Italy, Kazakhstan, Malaysia, Netherlands (Holland), New Zealand, Philippines, Poland, Russian Federation, Singapore, Slovenia, South Africa, Switzerland, Turkey, U.S.A., Ukraine, United Kingdom

www.maelearning.com

Introducing...
The Mastery Academy's E-Learning Center!

The Mastery Academy's goal has always been to share authentic knowledge of Chinese Metaphysics with the whole world.

Nevertheless, we do recognize that distance, time, and hotel and traveling costs – amongst many other factors – could actually hinder people from enrolling for a classroom-based course. But with the advent and amazing advance of IT today, NOT any more!

Convenient   Study from Your Own Home   Easy Enrollment

The Mastery Academy's E-Learning Center

Study at your own pace, and interact with your Instructor and fellow students worldwide, from anywhere in the world. With our E-Learning Center, knowledge of Chinese Metaphysics is brought DIRECTLY to you in all its clarity – topic-by-topic, and lesson-by-lesson; with illustrated presentations and comprehensive notes expediting your learning curve!

Welcome to **www.maelearning.com**; the web portal of our E-Learning Center, and YOUR virtual gateway to Chinese Metaphysics!

www.masteryacademy.com

Mastery Academy around the world

YAP GLOBAL CONSULTING

Joey Yap & Yap Global Consulting

Headed by Joey Yap, Yap Global Consulting (YGC) is a leading international consulting firm specializing in Feng Shui, Mian Xiang (Face Reading) and BaZi (Destiny Analysis) consulting services worldwide. Joey Yap - an internationally renowned Master Trainer, Consultant, Speaker and best-selling Author - has dedicated his life to the art and science of Chinese Metaphysics.

YGC has its main office in Kuala Lumpur, and draws upon its diverse reservoir of strength from a group of dedicated and experienced consultants based in more than 30 countries, worldwide.

As the pioneer in blending established, classical Chinese Metaphysics techniques with the latest approach in consultation practices, YGC has built its reputation on the principles of professionalism and only the highest standards of service. This allows us to retain the cutting edge in delivering Feng Shui and Destiny consultation services to both corporate and personal clients, in a simple and direct manner, without compromising on quality.

Across Industries: Our Portfolio of Clients

Our diverse portfolio of both corporate and individual clients from all around the world bears testimony to our experience and capabilities.

Virtually every industry imaginable has benefited from our services - ranging from academic and financial institutions, real-estate developers and multinational corporations, to those in the leisure and tourism industry. Our services are also engaged by professionals, prominent business personalities, celebrities, high-profile politicians and people from all walks of life.

YAP GLOBAL CONSULTING

Name (Mr./Mrs./Ms.):_____

Contact Details

Tel   :_____

Fax   :_____

Mobile :_____

E-mail :_____

What Type of Consultation Are You Interested In?
☐ Feng Shui   ☐ BaZi   ☐ Date Selection   ☐ Yi Jing

Please tick if applicable:
☐ Are you a Property Developer looking to engage Yap Global Consulting?

☐ Are you a Property Investor looking for tailor-made packages to suit your investment requirements?

Thank you for completing this form. Please fax it back to us at:

Malaysia & the rest of the world
Fax : +603-2284 2213   Tel : +603-2284 1213

---

www.joeyyap.com

www.joeyyap.com

Feng Shui Consultations

For Residential Properties
- Initial Land/Property Assessment
- Residential Feng Shui Consultations
- Residential Land Selection
- End-to-End Residential Consultation

For Commercial Properties
- Initial Land/Property Assessment
- Commercial Feng Shui Consultations
- Commercial Land Selection
- End-to-End Commercial Consultation

For Property Developers
- End-to-End Consultation
- Post-Consultation Advisory Services
- Panel Feng Shui Consultant

For Property Investors
- Your Personal Feng Shui Consultant
- Tailor-Made Packages

For Memorial Parks & Burial Sites
- Yin House Feng Shui

BaZi Consultations

Personal Destiny Analysis
- Personal Destiny Analysis for Individuals
- Children's BaZi Analysis
- Family BaZi Analysis

Strategic Analysis for Corporate Organizations
- Corporate BaZi Consultations
- BaZi Analysis for Human Resource Management

Entrepreneurs & Business Owners
- BaZi Analysis for Entrepreneurs

Career Pursuits
- BaZi Career Analysis

Relationships
- Marriage and Compatibility Analysis
- Partnership Analysis

For Everyone
- Annual BaZi Forecast
- Your Personal BaZi Coach

Date Selection Consultations

- **Marriage Date Selection**
- **Caesarean Birth Date Selection**
- **House-Moving Date Selection**
- **Renovation & Groundbreaking Dates**

- **Signing of Contracts**
- **Official Openings**
- **Product Launches**

Yi Jing Assessment

A Time-Tested, Accurate Science

• With a history predating 4 millennia, the Yi Jing - or Classic of Change - is one of the oldest Chinese texts surviving today. Its purpose as an oracle, in predicting the outcome of things, is based on the variables of Time, Space and Specific Events.

• A Yi Jing Assessment provides specific answers to any specific questions you may have about a specific event or endeavor. This is something that a Destiny Analysis would not be able to give you.

Basically, what a Yi Jing Assessment does is focus on only ONE aspect or item at a particular point in your life, and give you a calculated prediction of the details that will follow suit, if you undertake a particular action. It gives you an insight into a situation, and what course of action to take in order to arrive at a satisfactory outcome at the end of the day.

Please Contact YGC for a personalized Yi Jing Assessment!

Tel: +603-2284 1213   Email: consultation@joeyyap.com

www.joeyyap.com

Inviting us to Your Corporate Events

Many reputable organizations and institutions have worked closely with YGC to build a synergistic business relationship by engaging our team of consultants, led by Joey Yap, as speakers at their corporate events. Our seminars and short talks are always packed with audiences consisting of clients and associates of multinational and public-listed companies as well as key stakeholders of financial institutions.

We tailor our seminars and talks to suit the anticipated or pertinent group of audience. Be it a department, subsidiary, your clients or even the entire corporation, we aim to fit your requirements in delivering the intended message(s).

Tel: +603-2284 1213   Email: consultation@joeyyap.com

CHINESE METAPHYSICS REFERENCE SERIES

The Chinese Metaphysics Reference Series is a collection of reference texts, source material, and educational textbooks to be used as supplementary guides by scholars, students, researchers, teachers and practitioners of Chinese Metaphysics.

These comprehensive and structured books provide fast, easy reference to aid in the study and practice of various Chinese Metaphysics subjects including Feng Shui, BaZi, Yi Jing, Zi Wei, Liu Ren, Ze Ri, Ta Yi, Qi Men and Mian Xiang.

The Ten Thousand Year Calendar

The Chinese Metaphysics Compendium

Dong Gong Date Selection

The Date Selection Compendium

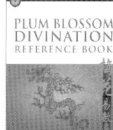
Plum Blossoms Divination Reference Book

Xuan Kong Da Gua Ten Thousand Year Calendar

Xuan Kong Da Gua Structures Reference Book

Xuan Kong Da Gua 64 Gua Transformation Analysis

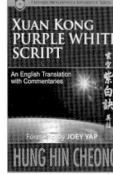
Xuan Kong Purple White Script

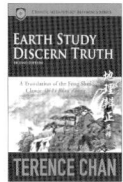
Earth Study Discern Truth Second Edition

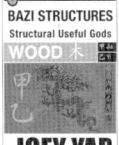
Bazi Structures and Structural Useful Gods - Wood

Bazi Structures and Structural Useful Gods - Fire

Bazi Structures and Structural Useful Gods - Earth

Bazi Structures and Structural Useful Gods - Metal

Bazi Structures and Structural Useful Gods - Water

+603 - 2284 8080

Books: Feng Shui for Homebuyers Series

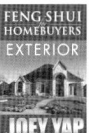 **Feng Shui For Homebuyers - Exterior**
(English & Chinese versions)

 **Feng Shui for Homebuyers - Interior**
(English & Chinese versions)

 **Feng Shui for Apartment Buyers - Home Owners**

Books: Stories and Lessons on Feng Shui Series

 **Stories and Lessons on Feng Shui**
(English & Chinese versions)

 **More Stories and Lessons on Feng Shui**

 **Even More Stories and Lessons on Feng Shui**

Continue Your Journey with Joey Yap's Books

 **Walking the Dragons**

 **Your Aquarium Here**

 **The Art of Date Selection: Personal Date Selection**

 **Xuan Kong Flying Stars Feng Shui**

 **Pure Feng Shui**

www.masteryacademy.com

Books: BaZi - The Destiny Code Series

 **BaZi - The Destiny Code** (English & Chinese versions)

 **BaZi - The Destiny Code Revealed**

Meet Your Day Master & Get To Know Yourself!

Find out your Day Master for FREE! **www.joeyyap.com/DM**

(English & Chinese versions)

The BaZi Essentials series of books comprise 10 individual books that focus on the individual Day Masters in BaZi (Four Pillars of Destiny, or Chinese Astrology) study and analysis. With each book focusing on one particular Day Master, Joey explains why the Day Master is the fundamental starting point for BaZi analysis, and is the true essence of one's character traits and basic identity.

With these concise and entertaining books that are designed to be both informative and entertaining, Joey shows how each person is different and unique, yet share similar traits, according to his or her respective Day Master. These 10 guides will provide crucial insight into why people behave in the various different ways they do.

+603 - 2284 8080

Books: Face Reading Series

 **Mian Xiang - Discover Face Reading** (English & Chinese versions)

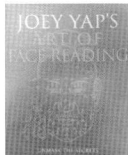 **Joey Yap's Art of Face Reading**

Easy Guide on Face Reading

All you need to know about the Eyes, Eyebrows, Mouth, Nose and Ears.

Joey Yap's brand new Face Reading Essentials Series are easy, fast, and effective guides for beginners, enthusiasts, and the curious. Learn to read your face by identifying the facial features on your own face, and the faces of the people around you.

These are EASY, FAST and EFFECTIVE guides for beginners, enthusiasts, and the curious. Make first impressions work for you by applying Face Reading skills to understand the personality and character of the person standing in front of you, whether at work, in business meetings, on a date, or anywhere else!

(English & Chinese versions)

www.masteryacademy.com

Annual Releases

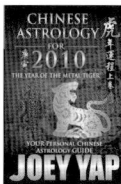
Chinese Astrology for 2010

Feng Shui for 2010

Weekly Tong Shu Diary 2010

Tong Shu Monthly Planner 2010

Tong Shu Desktop Calendar 2010

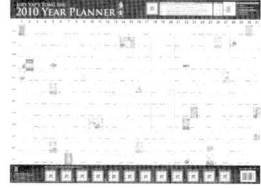
Tong Shu Year Planner 2010

+603 - 2284 8080

Educational Tools & Software

Xuan Kong Flying Stars Feng Shui Software
The Essential Application for Enthusiasts and Professionals

Highlights of the software include:
- Natal Flying Stars
- Monthly Flying Stars
- 81 Flying Stars Combinations
- Dual-View Format
- Annual Flying Stars
- Flying Stars Integration
- 24 Mountains

All charts will be are printable and configurable, and can be saved for future editing. Also, you'll be able to export your charts into most image file formats like jpeg, bmp, and gif.

Mini Feng Shui Compass

The Mini Feng Shui Compass is a self-aligning compass that is not only light at 100gms but also built sturdily to ensure it will be convenient to use anywhere. The rings on the Mini Feng Shui Compass are bi-lingual and incorporate the 24 Mountain Rings that is used in your traditional Luo Pan.

BaZi Ming Pan Software Version 2.0
Professional Four Pillars Calculator for Destiny Analysis

The BaZi Ming Pan Version 2.0 Professional Four Pillars Calculator for Destiny Analysis is the most technically advanced software of its kind in the world today. It allows even those without any knowledge of BaZi to generate their own BaZi Charts, and provides virtually every detail required to undertake a comprehensive Destiny Analysis.

Joey Yap Feng Shui Template Set

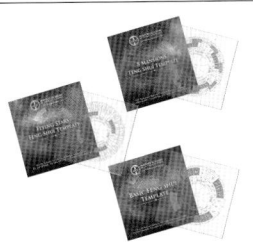

The Set comprises 3 basic templates: The Basic Feng Shui Template, 8 Mansions Feng Shui Template, and the Flying Stars Feng Shui Template.

Main Features:
- Easy-to-use, simple, and straightforward
- Small and portable; each template measuring only 5" x 5"
- Additional 8 Mansions and Flying Stars Reference Rings
- Handy companion booklet with usage tips and examples

www.masteryacademy.com

Feng Shui for Homebuyers DVD Series

In these DVDs, Joey will guide you on how to customise your home to maximise the Feng Shui potential of your property and gain the full benefit of improving your health, wealth and love life using the 9 Palace Grid. He will show you how to go about applying the classical applications of the Life Gua and House Gua techniques to get attuned to your Sheng Qi (positive energies).

    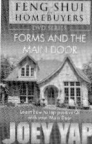 

Accelerate Your Face Reading Skills With Joey Yap's Face Reading Revealed DVD Series

In these highly entertaining DVDs, Joey will help you answer all these questions and more. You will be able to ascertain the underlying meaning of moles, birthmarks or even the type of your hair in Face Reading. Joey will also reveal the guidelines to help you foster better and stronger relationships with your loved ones through Mian Xiang.

+603 - 2284 8080

Discover Feng Shui with Joey Yap (TV Series) - Set of 4 DVDS

Discover Feng Shui with Joey Yap: Set of 4 DVDs

Informative and entertaining, classical Feng Shui comes alive in *Discover Feng Shui with Joey Yap!*

Dying to know how you can use Feng Shui to improve your house or office, but simply too busy attend for formal classes?

You have the questions. Now let Joey personally answer them in this 4-set DVD compilation! Learn how to ensure the viability of your residence or workplace, Feng Shui-wise, without having to convert it into a Chinese antiques' shop. Classical Feng Shui is about harnessing the natural power of your environment to improve quality of life. It's a systematic and subtle metaphysical science.

And that's not all. Joey also debunks many a myth about classical Feng Shui, and shares with viewers Face Reading tips as well!

Own the series that national channel 8TV did a re-run of in 2005, today!

Elevate Your Feng Shui Skills With Joey Yap's Home Study Course And Educational DVDs

Xuan Kong Vol.1
An Advanced Feng Shui Home Study Course

Feng Shui for Period 8 - (DVD)

Xuan Kong Flying Stars Beginners Workshop - (DVD)

BaZi Four Pillars of Destiny Beginners Workshop - (DVD)

www.masteryacademy.com

Interested in learning MORE about Feng Shui? Advance Your Feng Shui Knowledge with the Mastery Academy Courses.

Feng Shui Mastery Series™
LIVE COURSES (MODULES ONE TO FOUR)

The Feng Shui Mastery Series comprises Feng Shui Mastery Modules 1, 2, 3, and 4. It is a program that introduces students to the theories, principles, analyses, and interpretations of classical Feng Shui. It is a thorough, comprehensive program that covers important theories from various classical Feng Shui systems including Ba Zhai, San Yuan, San He, and Xuan Kong.

BaZi Mastery Series™
LIVE COURSES (MODULES ONE TO FOUR)

The BaZi Mastery Series comprises BaZi Mastery Modules 1, 2, 3, and 4 which provides students with a thorough introduction to BaZi, along with an intensive understanding of BaZi principles and the requisite skills to practice it with accuracy and precision. Students who complete these modules will be well-prepared to perform readings and interpretations. Feng Shui practitioners will also benefit from having knowledge of BaZi, as it will complement and enhance their Feng Shui practice.

+603 - 2284 8080

XUAN KONG MASTERY SERIES™
LIVE COURSES (MODULES ONE TO THREE)
* Advanced Courses For Master Practitioners

The Xuan Kong Mastery Series allows students to take their introductory steps into the captivating world of this powerful science. While Classical Feng Shui is always about the study of Location and Direction, Xuan Kong factors in the concept of Time into the equation as well. This course that will expose students to the extremely advanced techniques and formulas based upon those that were used by the ancient masters, as derived from the classics. It paves the way for students to specialize in the intelligent and strategic allocation of Qi, allowing them to literally manipulate Qi to assist in their life endeavours.

Mian Xiang Mastery Series™
LIVE COURSES (MODULES ONE AND TWO)

As one of the time-tested Five Arts (Wu Xing) of Chinese Metaphysics, Mian Xiang falls under the study of the physiognomy of the features, contours, shapes and hues of the face. In Mian Xiang, however, a person's face is more than what he or she shows the world; it's also a virtual map of this person's potential and destiny in life.

The Mian Xiang Mastery Series comprises Module 1 and Module 2 to allow students to learn this ancient art in a thorough, detailed manner. Each module has a carefully-developed syllabus that allows students to get acquainted with the fundamentals of Mian Xiang before moving on to the more intricate theories and principles that will enable them to practice Mian Xiang with greater depth and complexity.

www.masteryacademy.com

Yi Jing Mastery Series™
LIVE COURSES (MODULES ONE AND TWO)

'Yi' relates to change. Indeed, flux - or continuous change - is the key concept of the Yi Jing. Change is the only constant in life, and there is no exception to this rule. Evolution, transformation, alteration - call it by any other name, its effects are still far-reaching and encompasses every law - natural or manmade - known to our universe.

The Yi Jing Mastery Series provides an introductory look into the basics and fundamentals of Yi Jing thought and theory. As the Yi Jing functioned as an ancient Chinese oracle thousands of years ago, this Module will explore Yi Jing as a science of divination and probe the ways in which the concept of 'change' plays a big part in Yi Jing. Together both modules aim to give casual and serious Yi Jing enthusiasts a serious insight into one of the most important philosophical treatises in ancient Chinese thought.

Ze Ri Mastery Series™
LIVE COURSES (MODULES ONE AND TWO)

The ZeRi Mastery Series, or Date Selection, comprise two modules: ZeRi Mastery Series Module 1 and ZeRi Mastery Series Module 2. This program provides students with a thorough introduction to the art of Date Selection both for Personal and Feng Shui purposes. Both modules provide a fundamental grounding in all the rudimentary basics and allow you to move from the more straightforward techniques in Module 1 to the more sophisticated methods of Xuan Kong Da Gua in Module 2 with ease and confidence.

Feng Shui for Life

Feng Shui for life is a 5-day course designed for the Feng Shui beginner to learn how to apply practical Feng Shui in day-to-day living. It is a culmination of powerful tools and techniques that allows you to gain quick proficiency in Classical Feng Shui.

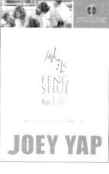

Mastery Academy courses are conducted around the world. Find out when will Joey Yap be in your area by visiting **www.masteryacademy.com** or call our office at **+603-2284 8080**.

+603 - 2284 8080